TWO PILLAR MAN

DAVID B. LOVEALL

David's humor will keep you off guard just before the principles of Two Pillars bring you to reality. His "Manly Man", "Tool Time" approach to life is exactly the underpinning of man's failing attempts to be like Christ. This book offers a fix for that "trouble code light" being on. I was shocked to learn of David's Rocket Incident and I am left wondering if the neighbors name is Jedidiah and a small bit of prophecy was fulfilled. If your walk with the Lord is in these preverbal gray areas, the Two Pillar Principals are exactly what you need as the instruction base for your daily walk.
CHUCH POOLE - MEN'S SMALL GROUP LEADER SADDLEBACK CHURCH

In 70 enjoyable pages laced with humor and substance, David Loveall has managed to encapsulate the essence of being a godly individual - living a life of Truth and Honor. His recounting of an escapade to which many of us can all too easily relate, was the perfect illustration for reminding us that accountability is something we can practice on earth that will have eternal consequences and benefits.
CEDRICK ADAMS - IT ENTREPRENEUR AND BUSINESSMAN

I believe men have allowed the Western church to become emasculated, which has caused it to be ineffective in the world today. David reminds us as men of our positions, not only in the church but as Husbands, Fathers and Leaders, any place we are called to love from. This book will provoke you, as it did me, to take a deeper look inward and ask God to wake up the places we've allowed to go to sleep. It's time as men to wake up and take our place! The best is yet to come!
BRUCE JACKMAN - INTERNATIONAL HOUSE OF PRAYER KANSAS CITY

This book needs to be on the desk of every policeman, government official even up to the President of every country. These two pillars can change the men who lead the world and thus change the world. This great change begins with you, and the opportunity to change, is in your very hands.
EDWARD MBUYI , BISHOP GOODWILL AFRICA MINISTRIES

TWO PILLAR MAN – THE GOSPEL OF THE ROCKET STORY

Copyright ©2016 by David B. Loveall, Author/Publisher
Requests for information should be sent to:
Three Sixteen Ministries Int'l
david@threesixteenministries.com

ISBN-13: 978-1522873631 CreateSpace, a DBA of On-Demand Publishing, LLC.
ISBN-10: 1522873635
BISAC: Religion / Christian Life / Men's Issues

The rocket story is the perfect setting for THE TWO PILLAR MAN test. Two massive pillars built at the entrance to Solomon's temple were powerful symbols of two God-ordained principles to walking uprightly. These bronze statements are designed to develop unwavering character against any attack and will bring truth into tempting compromises that are continually stripping away men's honor and respect.

"So I write that you may know how you ought to conduct yourself in the house of God, which is the church of the living God, the pillar and ground of the truth." 1 Timothy 3:15 NKJV

Even though you might have blown something up, it doesn't mean you have to blow it completely.

Scripture quotations from:
The New King James Version. Copyright © 1982 by Thomas Nelson, Inc. Used by permission. All rights reserved.
Holy Bible, New Living Translation, copyright ©1996, 2004, 2007, 2013, 2015 by Tyndale House Foundation. Used by permission of Tyndale House Publishers, Inc., Carol Stream, Illinois 60188. All rights reserved.
THE MESSAGE. Copyright © by Eugene H. Peterson 1993, 1994, 1995, 1996, 2000, 2001, 2002. Used by permission of NavPress. All rights reserved. Represented by Tyndale House Publishers, Inc.

All rights reserved. No part of this publication may be reproduced, stored in a retrieval system, or transmitted in any form or by any means-electronic, mechanical, photocopy, recording, or any other-except for brief quotations in printed reviews, without the prior permission of the publisher/author.

Cover design: Bethany Loveall, JULY NINE.com
Cover and inset photo: Loveallphoto.com
First Printing April 2016 / Printed in the U.S.A.

TWO PILLAR MAN
THE GOSPEL OF THE ROCKET STORY

DAVID B. LOVEALL

Dedicated to every man who realizes that what he ***speaks and does***...is everything.
Especially, that young boy who's now become a solid man of integrity, my firstborn son who stood with me at the door that day, watching.

DAVID B. LOVEALL

TABLE OF CONTENTS

INTRODUCTION

CHAPTER 1 – **MEN LIKE TO BLOW STUFF UP**

CHAPTER 2 – **THE CONCEPT OF TRUTH**

CHAPTER 3 – **WHAT FALLS FROM YOUR LIPS**

CHAPTER 4 – **METALLURGY OF A MAN**

CHAPTER 5 – **CRAMP OR SWIM, THE FIRST PILLAR**

CHAPTER 6 – **PAY UP, THE SECOND PILLAR**

CHAPTER 7 – **THE GOSPEL OF THE ROCKET STORY**

DAVID B. LOVEALL

INTRODUCTION

The desire and DNA of any man is to have access to reliable tools and ability to fix stuff if it breaks.

These are the simple basics to manhood.

They also represent the game-plan men adopt when it comes to the maintenance of their godly character. Get the right tools. Work and practice with those tools, as long as they offer progress. Fix it right the first time so we can continue to depend on the reliability of those tools in the future.

I've always thought that if a man could do this with biblical matters, he would be consistent in handling challenges to personal honor and integrity and be equipped to fight off the assault the enemy doles out daily to emasculate us.

There's no magic bullet to the daily protocol with regard to a man's godly character. (There might be a service manual, but what man would read it?) I always believed though, with all of my heart, that my God would have left a simple set of gizmos that all men could hang their tool belts on. A set of concepts or standards common to all men. Something simple. Sure. Dependable for every day. I just had to find it.

There must be a universal something in the Bible that every man could grab onto like he would his favorite socket. Perhaps even a pair of tools that, once put to use in each hand, would become so imprinted on his heart that they would become an ironclad set of principles to live life by. The kind of standards that would navigate every man through the step-by-step mazes when facing something compromising, broken, or shady. A set of guidelines that when applied, would guide every situation of honesty and relational integrity into restoration and wholeness.

Now some of you might say that kind of guidance is in the person of the Holy Spirit. And I would agree. But we men gotta' get to where that makes sense. Most men just don't adapt instantly, going from being "hands on" and "in control" to spiritual dependence. In my 50-plus years of living this out myself and being a pastor to men for the last 20, including inside prisons, I have found the obvious. Men are more literal than relational when it comes to working on those kind of spirit matters. We need a something first before we trust a someone.

I found that trying to delve into major spirit maintenance without some basic "tooling up" to get me closer in the spirit left me feeling as if I had a wrench ready, but no bolt to turn. My Christian walk began to feel like I was leaving too many loose parts scattered about my work area. I was unsure where they fit, and how much each needed to be tightened down.

Good intentions scattered my shop floor: rules and church traditions whose tools didn't seem to apply faithfully in every fix-it situation. Self-defeating expectations too, the "wish-a, could-a, why-didn't-I-dos" that never got me closer to assembling anything resembling solid, consistent spiritual character. I was constantly and aimlessly looking for something that could fix those constant leaks of character fluid.

While teaching men's groups over the past few decades, I realized that, generally, most men were having difficulty seeing the real truth and having the gut fortitude to *do* the action required of them. Especially in the little matters of life, when such tasks were misinterpreted as unimportant in the grand scheme of things, but later proved to be extremely important.

We men are still a capable breed for sure. God created us to be able to see a repair of any kind and get the job done. However, no man likes to bust and bloody his knuckles on cheap tools that don't work. Quality, God kind of tools are the kind that are tested and proven. Once we really latch onto to those kinds, we will use them again and again. Every job is easier with the right tools. Every motor runs better when it's been tuned the right way. Every man wants his motor to have serious VAROOM! Truth is, nobody wants to be a three-cylinder guy wimp in a V-8 world.

According to John 16, the Holy Spirit was put here to be a "guide into all truth," revealing what is to come and how to face it when it does. In other words, he's the spirit person whose job is to teach and mentor us into practicing the right thing to say and do, at the right time, for the right reasons. And because all of us are at different places in our growth journeys, the tools would have to fit all of us at every stage: for the young who are just learning how "righty-tighty" and "lefty-loosey" work to the mature who are working with full power, these tools must be pillars of immutable character that can lock down every man's ambition to be a steady God follower. Even if it's only one quarter turn at a time, and especially when the enemy throws a monkey wrench at us.

The tool-symbols I found were in the material and architecture of Solomon's temple: those big bronze pillars whose job it was to support the roof of the temple. They served as a symbol of strength and the truest establishment of Jehovah's word. They were monumental frames to the entrance into the holiest of holies, a gateway to God himself. They were a pair of gigantic, dual reminders of what kind of men we would all become if, and when, we made the decision to enter into what the Creator made for His created.

No man could be the same once he walked through those pillars and no man today who takes on their calling will be either. Back then, as it is today, a man would have to first agree with what the pillars stood for, or a man would have had no business even coming into the doorway. Their overbearing presence, by design, would overpower the weak and uncommitted.

These two pillars had names. And in the meanings of their names revealed to me the secret tools God intended to be carried by His men further repeated in other mighty men in other parts of the bible who were pillar-like. Pillars, by their construction and design are specifically engineered to "transmit, through compression, the weight of the structure above to the other structural elements below." Pillars then, transmit the weight, the presence and responsibilities of heaven from the Father through solid principles, to whatever they stand on. This is a reflection of what men do when they live like pillars.

As a man who has gone through the man stages from boyhood, cowboy, warrior, lover, king and now a living sage, I desired at each level to stand on the firmest of foundations. This, as we all know, is Jesus Christ. But, at the same time, I found myself constantly tempted to compromise and operate in some self-serving gray areas for the sake of self-protection. Those are the places where we tell those around us what pieces of the truth we think they can handle so it doesn't overly incriminate us to look bad or incapable and therefore, potentially unlikable.

It's like all of the times we men brag about forgotten hot exploits just so we can protect the truth of our present lukewarmness and failures.

This area of gray was never clearer until my wife and I had separated for a while when my son was just a year old. I had to face the fact that there was so much of my honor and character that had been compromised into believing I was still an "OK honest kind of guy," but the truth was, I wasn't. I had to willfully seek these go-to instruments of righteous guidance and put them into practice in my daily routine. Full truth. Doing what I say. Being who I claimed to be. I needed these solid black and white principles to ward off the increasing grayness. I needed a brace to lean on that would always be true and right. One that would always act as tandem supports to my (at the time) struggling faith.

It's been well over a decade now practicing these two pillar principles. They've changed me drastically and have been faithful in keeping me steered back toward the right at every test. They've also repaired thousands of men to whom I have shared their profound concepts. Men who earnestly wanted to fix something deep within themselves, but just lacked the reliable starter tools that another man would pass down to them.

That is, until now.

Jachin and Boaz stood as two pillars of monumental truth, action and bulletproof integrity. Now they serve as tools to remind us that every man can gain not only good standing with God, but become a continually better man of character who can be relied on to make something right.

Not all of us can strip down and build a race-ready V-8 or cover ourselves in deer urine and shoot dinner with a bow and arrow. Heck, I couldn't grow a mustache until I was nearly forty, but I tell you this…with these pillars, every man can build a solid character that will reward him with confidence, faith and respect.

Even if he finds himself with stuff that's broken.

DAVID B. LOVEALL

CHAPTER 1 – **MEN LIKE TO BLOW STUFF UP**

It was late summer. We were cleaning up from the last potential backyard barbeque of the season. The energy from the hot dogs and hamburgers were fading and the party needed a little pick-me-up or at least, a last-season send-off.

Months prior, on a family road trip out of state, we passed by a firework stand with a gigantic sign overhead that read, "Big Rockets." Although outlawed in the state where I'm from, I couldn't resist my kiddish impulse. I quickly pulled off the road and scored me a beast-like space specimen. I had it wrapped tightly in a brown paper bag and hid it deep in my trunk near the spare tire for the long trip back home—and then forgot about it.

How I remembered the stashed rocket on that fateful day of our last barbeque is still a mystery, but when I pulled the colossal, colorful cylinder with the long red stick out of my trunk, mischievous giddiness washed over me.

We live in the suburbs, houses packed together like bowling balls in an egg carton. So if we were going to set off this bodacious rocket, we needed to make sure it was going to go straight up. It had to miss the power lines behind us and, of course, all of the houses around us.

Ingenuity kicked in. I found a four-foot section of plastic gutter from my last fix-it project. Between my 10-year-old son and me, we cobbled up some two-by-four braces and leaned them against the picnic table. It created a NASA-designed chute to send the bomb-on-a-stick into the sky.

I glanced over the fence, making sure no neighbors were watching. The coast was clear. I lit the fuse.

Those brief moments of anticipation were breath-taking. My son blurted out a girlie squeal the instant the rocket's fuse ignited the first stage. A ten-foot fire-trail funneled out of the rain gutter as the rocket cleared our makeshift launch tower for the wild blue yonder. "WHHOOOOOOSH!" It sped off so fast I barely got the words "wow" off my lips.

A millisecond after take-off, as if it had been reprogrammed, the explosive shuttle pulled an abrupt u-turn and zoomed toward the ground. It narrowly missed the 12-foot arborvitae hedge at the rear of our property and zoomed recklessly lower, barely clearing the roof line on the house behind ours. *Houston, we have a problem.*

There was an unexpected delay, almost as if it was going to be a dud, then, an explosion that reverberated across the entire neighborhood. It shook the windows in our house. Right after, a panicked, blood-curdling scream came as the "boom" echoed a second time. The shriek sounded like it came from way beyond, over the back house roof, maybe even the next street over.

"Oh, my God!" a man yelled just after the first scream subsided, and then, subsequent commotions from other neighbors added to the abrupt pandemonium. Apparently, some kind of triage was happening over yonder. People were hustling about with air-raid urgency.

My son and I read each other's mortified faces. We quickly gathered up the launching pad evidence, stowed the wood braces, and the soot-stained gutter section. We fox-holed into the house. We locked the door behind us, snickering at first, then plopping ourselves on the sofa in gut-busting laughter.

"Did you hear some sort of boom?" asked my wife

"Yeah, but couldn't tell where it came from," I said.

My son shrugged his shoulders in agreement.

Self protection. We some kind of bad boys because we blow stuff up, yeah, and got off apparently Scot-free. Gray area.

The fact is, right after something explodes, truth and blame go in completely opposite directions. When it comes to the truth, it's either blown out of proportion, or blown off entirely, for the sake of self preservation. That's why we hid in the house. It was fun and the belief that fun things only have bad consequences if blame is leveled by some one, well, un-fun. That's why blame goes in a completely different direction than truth, because it's trying to hide something. It takes the eyes off the real truth and, if executed properly, might save the reputation of the one who ignited the fuse and caused the explosion in the first place.

Three months later, the incident all but forgotten, a knock came on our door. Through the frosted glass I saw a man. No brown package. No uniform. No smile.

"What the?" I wondered.

My son beat me to the door by a step and was standing to my right as I swung it open with it's signature squeak.

"Hello, my name is." And just like the sounds when Charlie Brown's teacher speaks when he's about to be schooled, all I heard was a string of indiscernible blah, blah, blah until those piercing specifics: "I've been on vacation in Hawaii for the past three months, and when I came back, my dining room window was all boarded up from being blown out. There was also a major black stain on the side of my house.

"I asked around and some of the neighbors said you might have been setting off some fireworks while I was gone, and I just wanted to know. "

To which he thrusts a broom-handle sized red stick with the blackened cylinder end detonated beyond recognition. "By chance, is this your bottle rocket?"

With this damning piece of evidence hanging inches from my face, he awaited my response. There followed, as one might expect, an extended moment of awkward silence.

There were only two of us at the entrance to my house who knew the complete truth. The third had a pretty good idea and was waiting for a confirmation of my integrity from the evidence he had already gathered. Court was over. The prosecution had all the evidence required for a conviction. All that was left was a case-ending confession before sentencing. The next move was mine.

I considered a polite lie, then closing the door on the man—and the incident—without consequences. It wasn't my fault the rocket didn't travel skyward as advertised. I bought and launched a rocket not a ground mortar. After all, he couldn't prove anything. There's no DNA. For crying out loud, it was three months ago. Isn't there some statute of limitations for firework foul-ups? Heck, I, too, could've even been on vacation!

Or there was the other choice. The consciousness and realization that this was a holy moment about to unfold, which would put to the test all of the integrity I've espoused as a dad toward my son. And as a man.

What kind of pillars held my personal house up? All of my talk of being honest and doing the right thing were now meeting the test of a lifetime. My next utterance would determine what kind of man I really was: A guy who only gives lip service to the calling? Or one who would answer boldly in the face of potential conviction? Also, what precedent would be laid down in that moment in front of my first born, 10-year-old son? What response would serve to set the foundation for his future?

It was pillar time.

CHAPTER 2 – **THE CONCEPT OF TRUTH**

WHAT IS TRUTH? I mean really.

"Truth? Well, that depends. Are we talking mine? Or yours?"

Anytime a man is facing rocket-damming truth, is also when there's a potential of it costing. Reputation. Pride. Someone dipping deep into the checkbook. Plus, there's the humiliating scolding that might come with full disclosure. So "that depends" is that moment in which truth is interpreted and practiced by each man. It must have a baseline and become the basis to what kind of truth we're talking about now, doesn't it?

As a concept, truth has always been, and will always be, a moving target. Your truth? Or my truth? Does truth come about when we agree? Or when it's convenient for both of us to get what we want? Or is truth a gray interpretation, a way we can deflect improvable culpability away from what *is*, while pinning someone else with its consequences so it doesn't come back on us. Real truth is naked exposure, which we naturally try to avoid at all costs. Men don't do the Full Monty when it comes to the prospect of dishonor.

For example, consider a man caught in adultery. It might seem best to keep the full details hidden; that way, if he's crafty enough, he can actually turn the tables and make it look like it's someone else's fault. If partial and selectively revealed truth was skillfully laid, he might even be able to make it look like he was in fact, the victim.

Other questions beg for answers. Should the real truth always be divulged, even if it can't be proven? If there isn't enough evidence to fully convict, am I obligated by some sense of honor and character to be wholly transparent? Is it OK to dilute the truth enough with mere scraps of honesty so that I can make a "no contest" kind of admittance and not be looked at as wholly dishonest—especially in situations where indisputable evidence is being displayed on your front porch, in front of your kid?

Truth. What is truth? Pilate asked the question that's been echoing for centuries when he, in a moment of great desire for discernment, asked about the 'concept' of truth. When Jesus was being led to the crucifixion, Pilate pulls him aside in an attempt to sift through all the conjecture and accusations and get to the brass nuts.

"What is truth?" he asked to the face of Jesus. Essentially he was asking, "Who's adaptation should I be lining myself up with to make this crucial next decision rightly?"

Crowds screamed one version, the high priests declared another, Pilate's wife whispered a third, and the mob shouted a fourth: "Kill him! He's a liar. He claims to be God!" The high priests were relying on their unstated reputation of being representatives of the law-abiding truth, saying "of course he's worthy of death, why would we have brought him to you if he wasn't?"

Real, absolute clear truth was being realized slowly by all the participants. The wife of Pilate, who had no horse in this race, had been agonized in dreams prior to the moment at which the man standing at their doorstep, bound and whipped like a liar, was indeed speaking the complete truth. Pilate was, in his gut, coming to a new sense of "true North", because every bit of evidence suggested Jesus wasn't guilty of anything.

It's no wonder Pilate asked Jesus where the needle should be pointing because all hands of the truth compass were pointing different directions.

If Pilate had only heard what Jesus spoke just a few chapters earlier about truth, he would have known the answer to his pressing question. The "concept" of truth isn't a concept, it's a person. It's the guy who was standing right in front of his nose, with blood dripping from his forehead and indisputable words from his lips.

In fact, right after saying that He was going away to build a place for his disciples, Jesus told Thomas and the rest of his "guys," *"I am the way, the TRUTH and the life. No one can come to the Father except through me."* (John 14:6 NLT) Jesus plainly states here that truth is not a concept, a principle, a set of rules or a way of living. Truth is a person. Truth is Him. Jesus Christ.

Nearly half the references in the Bible about truth are in the book of John. Jesus demonstrated by his life and fulfillment of so many prophecies, that truth must always be irrefutable and undeniably bullet-proof when compared to Himself. Truth was proven by the life He walked and it can't be altered after the fact for the sake of cultural relevance or convenient interpretations. John writes at the end of the book that there was so much more "truth" Jesus lived that there wouldn't be books enough to contain the volume of proof from the person who defined it.

Without Jesus as the person of truth shaping a man's spiritual starting point, truth gets replaced by law. The person of truth gets replaced by varying concepts. The problem is, everyone breaks the law. Just ask every passenger who has ever ridden in my car. Though I've often bragged about being a law abiding citizen in an attempt to look more honest, fact is, I speed, habitually.

So the gray area of truth men create around themselves is this attempt to arrange a likable concept of truth under the varying degrees of how they keep laws that are acceptable to some standard. The concept that if a man keeps the biggies, then he must be a high scorer in the truth pavilion. Yet if he is lax in what he deems lesser important matters, promises to do lunch, call you and catch up, those rarely kept off the cuff stuff, he still finds somehow a score that is acceptable as an overall average that fits a self-serving concept.

What continues to gnaw at us even in the face of shifting values is an unrelenting spirit of truth that wants to find a solid place to land. We were made by God to want to do things right. Fortunately, there's still a way to get to God and back to right, through the Son. That's why John further quotes Jesus saying, *"But the time is coming—indeed it's here now—when true worshipers will worship the Father in spirit and in truth. The Father is looking for those who will worship him that way. For God is Spirit, so those who worship him must worship in spirit and in truth."* (John 4:23-24 NLT)

So, by looking at this truth-as-a-person thing, when we men get to know the nature and character of Jesus, who walked in honest truth, we learn absolute and immovable truth from his spirit and his nature. When men align themselves with the only version of truth that's never going to change, then solid, dependable growth in living truth is achieved. We become free of the altered concepts of truth and their deception.

Jesus received honor and respect from the Father, but He also received freedom. Freedom from not having to figure out the latest version of what Truth was or to see if His beliefs fit into current culture. He was it. Jesus made the standards and the framework and both were flawless.

"You will know the TRUTH and the TRUTH will set you free." (John 8:32 NKJ) By knowing what is real and unchanging, (the person of Christ), the promise is complete freedom. Not the irresponsible, dodgy "doesn't-apply-to-me" kind of freedom or "I got away with something I shouldn't have" kind of freedom, but a single brand which would work in every situation, for every man, every time.

"… So he explained to them: *'I tell you the TRUTH, **I am** the gate for the sheep.'"*

This statement bull's eyes the moving target thing. If a man wants to get into heaven, it's only through Christ. *Through the man of truth.* Not by living some brand of right morality. If a man desires to align his life with the truth and be considered such, he must learn to practice what the person of truth does. He must grab with both hands the tools that emulate Christ at every opportunity. Especially in situations when the opportunity comes calling to test him, on his own front porch, with the remains of a bottle rocket that was once his.

So what do I say to this guy on my porch waving a charred stick in my face? Is that my rocket? Well hell, yes! If I told the real, un-slanted truth, it's a dang certainty this is going to end up costing me dearly, which is exactly how God prepares a man to be a two-pillar man: when doing so might cost us something big, both in dollars and reputation.

If I'm going to strive or claim to be *that kind of a man*, then I'm going to have to speak all the truth, even when it's the hardest. By doing this first, I will be set up for, and pass, the rest of the test.

Indie Rock band, The Frey, once sang a lyric that, "the right thing and the hardest thing are the same." I knew I was about to sing a different tune than what was usual.

My neighbor also expected something from me that day on my porch. He expected me not to be a liar. He expected me to be a man who doesn't shrink back from the basic pillar standards that we all want to believe is a basic standard in all of us.

Ephesians 4:25 in the Message reminded me in that very moment, *'What this adds up to, then, is this: no more lies, no more pretense.* **Tell your neighbor the truth.** *In Christ's body we're all connected to each other, after all. When you lie to others, you end up lying to yourself.'*

I knew the lies I could tell myself would eventually ask a price. Deep down, the desire was there to do the right thing at the right time for the right reason. This way I can look myself in the mirror and honestly answer the question, "Do I speak the truth?" or "Am I an honest guy?" and not be lying to myself every time I catch my reflection. I hate being a hypocrite, or worse yet, admitting that I am one.

Given this opportunity, Jesus would speak only one thing, even unto death. Thus, as I faced my neighbor, I had no other choice if I wanted to attain the sturdier benefits of the pillars and stand like one.

Pillar number one's name at the entrance to the temple was Jachin, which means the (name of Jehovah) will be firmly established. What would be set in mortar here would depend on my next few words.

They would either be the straight truth kind of words that would force me to accept the cards as they fell. Or they would be a complicated smoke screen of deception and dodgy dialogue, proving only my duplicity.

I readied myself to face *the* truth.

CHAPTER 3 – **WHAT FALLS FROM YOUR LIPS**

If you have to tell me you're honest, you're not.

If I say to you, "You have my word," what do you have? Is that a promise? A vow? Or just a temporary good feeling of my assurances that I have no intention of fulfilling?

Words of promise, if they are rarely or minimally acted upon, become like a Lego block wall of oaths, lots of colorful segments that fit together nicely in our minds, but never meeting the expectations of the ones we spoke them to. We all want to believe statements of pledges we get from others, and they, too want to take stock in what we say. But unfortunately, most people never meet the bar of honor they profess. They lack a foundational standard of understanding to the power of their words.

Like when we casually say to a friend, "I'll call you" or "Let's do lunch" and then never do. What we're really doing is trying to make ourselves feel better about our lack of spending time with said person. We want the feeling the relationship is good but we are actually destroying it with an empty promise. That is the truth. Those words spoken become broken trust because you didn't make those statements into action.

In our harried culture, people loosely dispense words as part of quickly moving to the next event. This has only added to the volume of their worthlessness because we forget what we've put out there. Words out of our mouths have lost their brick-and-mortar standards. A standard that used to be like the old 1950's axiom, "my word is my bond". Iron clad candor like this has given way to "I couldn't keep up with the madness"... uh, sorry.

I've caught myself saying "yes I'll do" or "sure I'll be there" on the run to so many people that those commitments never got written down on my calendar. Hence, I forget. Then I unintentionally let someone down because they were counting on my actions. I then find myself making more statements of intended truth that I can't possibly keep up with.

I'm talking about even the basic kinds of words like, saying you'll meet a person at 2 p.m. and instead, shuffle in closer to 2:35, thinking "it's no-big-deal" kind of words.

If we viewed each word spoken as a brick, mortared into a solid covenant, (which is a promise between two people broken only by death), then our words wouldn't be so casual. They wouldn't have a certain percentage of noncommittal, which then makes them eventually, unbelievable.

Many times I've tried to re-right the words that have come out of my mouth, because at every level, I've got to be accountable to them. All of them. Even those which were jokes spoken just to be funny or to break the ice in awkward social settings. Many of those have come back to bite me in the butt.

The gospel of Matthew continues to remind me of this countless times: *"Let me tell you something: Every one of these careless words is going to come back to haunt you. There will be a time of Reckoning. Words are powerful; take them seriously. Words can be your salvation. Words can also be your damnation."* (Matthew 12:36-37 MSG)

Even when putting forth a determined effort to think before I speak, my mouth can betray me. Many times, it blurts out more trouble than it can back-peddle out of. I do, though, still try to be a man of all my pledges, especially in the important stuff, the stuff that's sworn on, agreed by notarized seals or assured by some other means of official declaration. Most of us men pride ourselves on keeping those kinds of vows, because signed contracts have our names attached to the them and are enforceable, and affect our credit rating.

The stuff without paperwork, however, gets lumped into the "the smaller stuff" category. Stuff that really shouldn't matter if it was just spoken, and then not carried out. Because in our minds they were just conversation, and small words at that, right? Yet to someone else, every little word uttered matters, because of the level of trust they've put in us. Little, insignificant promises become the foundation of large bonds of covenants that can hold in the balance great amounts of trust between another person whom I say I value. And that's especially true in the small stuff.

The writer of Proverbs says words can kill or give life. They're either poison or good fruit. I choose. If I choose to do what my words have spoken, then my life becomes one of good fruit. Anything less is poison, in me and in what comes out of me.

The Book of Deuteronomy, a retelling of God's laws to Moses and the Israelites, speaks deeply about truth. In Chapters 22-24, Moses was teaching about the practice of making vows.

"That which has gone from your lips you shall keep and perform, for you voluntarily vowed to the Lord your God what you have promised with your mouth." (Deuteronomy 23:23 NKJ)

Do you get this? Every word you speak is a vow. All spoken words are covenants. All my verbiage to another constitutes promises to God and the person they were spoken to.

Later, Jesus reminds us that our words are the overflow of our hearts. So if my heart has no intention of being completely true, and I speak idle words of promise or nice-sounding honor all day long, but don't deliver, I'm a vow breaker. I'm a living liar and by definition can't be trusted.

My words of inaction become just one long strand of unbelievable details, like our local TV weatherman who talks so fast with so many important weather words that it sounds like his whole forecast, is one long, babbling word of insignificance.

As I said before, these words spoken are weighty even in the simplest of covenants, like being on time for an appointment.

Recently in Uganda, teaching men's conferences, we hammered hard this point to all the men who were habitually late.

Nearly every church service I've been to limps along for three to five hours because the culture and the pastors have given permission for people to be slack in their honoring of time. I have been told by Ugandan bishops that if we start on time, no one will come. So those few who show up nearly on time must endure hours of dancing and singing introductions long enough for those who choose to be late, so they can arrive and be a part of church service. This is maddening for me. Why should those who dishonor others rule the day?

Here's what we taught at these men's conferences: when someone agrees to meet you at a certain time, they're giving you a slice of their lives, a slice they can never get back. If that time is not honored, we have dishonored the giver of that time.

Near the end of the first day of teaching, I repeated that our next day's start time was precisely at 9 a.m., hoping this concept would sink in.

"So, what time will you be here?" I asked repeatedly, like a high school cheerleader trying to stir the crowd. Most of the pastors and men mumbled under their breath as they struggled to answer the rally cry.

"To be on time you all will be here by 8:50 a.m., right?" I said over and over. The men slowly began to respond like a sports team, chanting with fist pumps and testosterone camaraderie. Yeah! We were making progress. *So I thought.*

As the Tarzan chest thumping died down, one smartly dressed man right in front of me piped up. On his jacket lapel was prominently pinned a large, laminated card that read "pastor." He had one weathered hand on his Bible, and one in the air waiting to be called on like a grade-schooler.

"I will be here, pastor, tomorrow at 11:30," he said brashly — and, I felt, a touch defiantly. That time was just before we serve the free lunch.

A few laughs and grunts peppered through the gathering. I came right up into the man's grill, like a drill sergeant, hoping to make a point about being on time and if need be, use him as an example. Maybe I'd even make him drop down and give me twenty just for messing up my momentum.

"Who does your math?" I bellowed over the stymied silence from the rest. "Does your cell phone tell time. Or is it broken?"

This was a prime opportunity to illustrate how not keeping your word, even about small things like time, can create a culture of disillusionment and distrust.

"Why would you be here at 11:30, right before lunch, when you know we are starting a very important lesson right at nine in the morning?"

My singling him out got the rest of the men stirred up to repeat the right answer. But sure enough, even with all the guilt and peer pressure I could heap on, that man showed up the next morning promptly at 11:30, just as he said he would.

Though he was late by my standards, and missed the critical lesson that second morning, I had to shake my head with a certain level of respect. He did do what he said he would. Even if I didn't like it. He kept his word that he spoke, even under severe peer pressure from many recruits who said they would be on time, which, if I'm being honest here, out of 50 men, only seven were. It's still a work in progress, boot camp ain't over though.

It takes courage to keep your word. This pastor who showed up late had his reasons. He was already committed and convicted to keep what fell from his lips to others he spoke prior to the conference. The important point here is when a man knows his words are vows, he will keep them. And many times, when a man is in this spiritual mindset to keep all of his words, he will keep even those foolish ones spoken against the grain or off the cuff. At that point, he will honor whatever he spoke, even at the risk of reputation and good standing, just to keep striving to a higher level of integrity. Or he will learn the higher lesson of not shooting his mouth off by trying to speak what he thinks people want to hear, and then leaving them hanging.

"Again, the law of Moses says, 'You shall not break your vows to God but must fulfill them all.' But I say: Don't make any

vows! And even to say 'By heavens!' is a sacred vow to God, for the heavens are God's throne. And if you say 'By the earth!' it is a sacred vow, for the earth is his footstool. And don't swear 'By Jerusalem!' for Jerusalem is the capital of the great King. Don't even swear 'By my head!' for you can't turn one hair white or black. Say just a simple 'Yes, I will' or 'No, I won't.' Your word is enough. To strengthen your promise with a vow shows that something is wrong." (Matthew 5:33-37 TLB)

As you can see, it takes the same size huevos to say "yes" and do what you say, as it does in saying "no" and refusing doing something in the first place. When a man stands by his words which have the gravity of covenants, then he can be trusted in every situation. And better than even being trusted, he can be respected. Always.

So if a "vow" is a covenant (according to Deuteronomy 23 an agreement unbroken except by death) anything that falls from our lips, as a casual promise is the same even if we don't wrap it in an airtight Ziploc baggie by saying, "I promise."

So then, if we speak it and preach it, we must walk in it. Even and especially if it gets inconvenient, or is too messy or erodes some prideful image of ourselves. By slogging through some of the past messes we've created, we're learning the value and impact of all of our words and keeping them, like real men do.

Words we deem self-defending, which are really complaining and comparing, have their costly paybacks too. Near the end of the book of Job, the mountain of statements between him, his friends and God has risen to the throne of heaven. With so much dissertation, he's making his case and requesting God to explain why he was unjustly punished. Finally, the Almighty responds:

"The Lord went on: "Do you still want to argue with the Almighty? Or will you yield? Do you—God's critic—have the answers?" Then Job replied to God: "I am nothing—how could I ever find the answers? I lay my hand upon my mouth in silence. I have said too much already." (Job 40:1-5 TLB)

The very next thing God tells Job is to "prepare yourself like a man, I will question you and you shall answer me." In other words, stand up like a man and face the coming battle of the words you spewed. Those words you foolishly spoke are coming back for a fight not to wipe you out, but for a lesson in being responsible wholly for the words you uttered. Man up. Take the punches. Get off the ground and walk wiser.

As I prepared my response to my neighbor on my porch, I gulped. It was a perfect time to find that already deposited shred of strength, to "man up." Be the man, Be the Boaz. The other pillar of the temple. Be his words too.

After all, my son was looking on, hanging upon my every word.

CHAPTER 4 – **METALLURGY OF A MAN**

"Now Concerning the Pillars."
Size does matter.
So does what they're made of, so does the placement, and so does the mass, which becomes the irrefutable message.

I'm not a big guy. I'm not like some of my friends who alter the temperature of a room just by standing in it. Average height these days is considered to be around five-foot nine-inches. Well, I'm a healthy horse hand below that. They're all kinds of reasons to be disappointed in those numbers, but none that I can do anything about. I've seen guys like me with "short-man's complex", but also others with "tall men's complex" or still others with a sundry of other "complexes." So I guess we're all about evenly sized then, in spirit construction and complexity.

Each adopted complex serves, however, to give reason (or blame) for the way we speak and act. All of which attempt to help us explain and answer one of the most basic man questions, "what makes me, me?" Blaming our manly make-up on what we've become and settled for from our environment is really saying that we're disappointed with what we've stood and still stand for. It's a position which apparently hasn't been working as well as we'd thought.

As a result, men have not risen to the bar of their God-given potential and design. Instead, they've sunk to what those other (shaky idol) busy-life pillars or adversity have produced.

The pillars that stood at the entrance to Solomon's temple were incredibly massive statements of God's promises and support to His people. They were also a grand set of symbols as to what men would become who entered into God's presence. They represented, in a huge way, what it meant to stand as a man of God in His church, passing through the entrance of pillar character into a very holy place.

Men, by God's own design, are crucial to the church. Let me say that again, men are crucial to Christ's church. Paul says they're the head of the household and urged to treat (and support) their wives like Christ does with His church. Spiritual order of authority flows this way. Blessings come forth from the Father, through the Son, through the men, and on through the rest of the family in which he is overseer. Pastors the world over have stated that, "if you get the men, you get the rest", meaning that if the men find their place (which are to be the pillars of the church) and they stand and receive what comes from the Son and Father, then the family of men, including the next generations of growing men, will find their place in the church, too.

The two temple pillars were built by Hiram. He was a widow's son, whose father was a skilled metal worker with great wisdom. He received all of his father's knowledge, enabling Hiram to construct two colossal statements about the grandeur and glory of the God of Israel. By their very construction, placement and substance, the two pillars reflected God's promises and covenant connection to the men of God, who would come to worship the one and only true God.

Men, then, are designed to be pillar-like. There were other smaller pillars erected in scripture built to stand as a reminder to men of the victory and promise made between men and God. They were also used to mark significant works of God in certain places. They marked miracles and stood as reminders of agreements with His people. So the pillars that Hiram got the design for were going to be the largest statements of those facts in history. Being a pillar man means you're going to be required to stand by and make these kinds of statements, from the boardroom, bedroom, or even on your front porch.

The pillars represented two important and ever present foundational markers of God's promises. These are the same traits that godly men were reminded of when they chose to walk in agreement with the Lord as their God. I imagine it being a most humbling and overwhelming experience walking up to and through the nearly 120 foot tower-like front entrance. A man had to do some serious soul-searching to see if he was even eligible to gain such access. He faced a daunting sense of accountability to hold himself to what those two pillars stood for, which were grand principles of faith and truth, vital commitments to action.

The pillars were cast in bronze, a material of utilitarian perseverance. Bronze was actually a strong mix of metals, nearly impossible to break apart. By many estimations they were nearly 30 feet high and six feet in diameter. They were hollow, the walls three to four inches thick, "four fingers" to a man. They were beyond stout. More solid than anything constructed previously.

The one placed at the Southern position (left) was named Jachin, meaning "firmly establish" referring to the person of Jehovah. The pillar to the North, (right) named Boaz, which means "in strength". So if you were to "read" the spiritual pillar implications in the style of the time (from right to left) the imposing message at the entrance would have been "May (Jehovah) firmly establish (the Temple) in strength".
(1 Kings 7:15-21 NKJ)

So in order to still answer the calling for men now to carry the torch of Christ into the world, we too need to be "firmly establishing Jehovah's word and acting toward His church in strength." We must continue striving to be men who talk and walk with the bronze-like integrity followed by conduct worthy to enter into the house of the living God, which is "the pillar and ground of the truth". (1Tim3:15 NKJ)

Other references to men who "were said to be pillars" (apostles James, Cephas, and John) (Gal 2:9) were those who stood up to mentor and bless Paul and Barnabas when they were sent out in the Gentile mission field. They were referenced as ones who were strong and firmly established men of the church. Ones who did what they said, and also those who trained other men to become pillars-like themselves.

Likewise, Christians, men and women who, in general, conquer over evil and overcome daily onslaughts to their faith, are made into "pillars in the temple of God" (Rev 3:12). They'll never have to leave the place where He dwells, because they beat the enemy on the battlefield by the promise and authority from the Son. They will be getting new names, names that mean something very significant and true. They will become citizens in the new Jerusalem and be given a personal, new identity from God himself. Pillar kind of character was always designed to lead us toward God, strengthen us through weak circumstances and give us credibility to mentor the next generation of men.

Sadly though, the original cast pillars that were set in the front of the temple didn't stand as long as they were designed. Somewhere along the way those symbols of God's firmly established word and strength broke down among the men who claimed they followed God, but with limited loyalty. The pillars were systematically decimated starting with just a few white lies. One un-kept word too small to deem important. One vow not fulfilled. One honorable deed promised but dishonored with laziness. Soon the men "firmly established in word and strength" had turned their loyalties one excuse or cover-up at time to gods that didn't even have names. Just like what is happening today.

We pick up the horrific news in Jeremiah chapter 52 just after the Chaldeans carried off the indestructible pillars piece by piece to Babylon. "The bronze pillars that *WERE* in the house of the Lord…were broke into pieces…the two pillars were beyond measure…Now concerning the pillars."

If we men don't pay immediate attention to this "concerning the pillars" statement, (i.e. shoring up our own pillars of moral standards), then we will certainly be witness to our own nation being broken apart by invaders and carried off. Bit-by-bit compromise to the truth and morality will dismantle sound character, allowing it to be discarded as cheap. It starts first with men and then flows down to the family.

Where are the pillars of men these days? They're tough to find because each man has made various brands of his own truth, which changes the framework for God's, so that the true immovable standards are getting lost. Those original pillars were large enough to get our attention. Thirty two feet tall and twelve feet around. You couldn't miss them or the statements they spoke through their mass. But they were also simply designed to be immovable, set in one place, so a man's own shifting-ness couldn't change their position. The only thing a man could do was to turn his back on them. We have the same choice today.

Closing the door on my neighbor and again hiding in my house would have been turning my back on those pillars. They were massively in my face. The sheer size of the problem was potentially getting larger by the minute. If I admitted to the ownership of the rocket, who knows where that truth might take me? But if I didn't, I'd be turning my back on another opportunity of gaining character.

In an attempt to find new standards to fit with changing ideology and morality, we've allowed these bronze standards to be broken apart. Bit by bit our passivity and lack of courage have destroyed a standard to do what is truly right. Shrinking back into the safety nets of tolerance and political correctness has limited ourselves to be too ill-equipped to do the works of God when we've tried to cast our nets on the other side of the boat or into uncharted waters.

When men have chosen to live by any other set of standards, not designed as part of the "temple" architecture, what we end up building is an entrance into holy places that lacks solid curb appeal. It doesn't even attract our family or those that are a part of our assigned circle of influence. Because our benchmarks of checking our integrity are somewhat gray and lacking clear guidelines, we make the word of God and His church unappealing, hypocritical. It is unapproachable because the church, based on our words and actions, is considered worthless and undependable. It's just another moving target. Thanks, but I'll aim elsewhere.

A handful of men pillars have repeated over the years what Edmund Burke stated about shrinking back from rock solid principles and mere intentions of doing good. He said "the only thing necessary for the triumph of evil is for good men to do nothing."

Each man must then decide to do something if we are going to rally back to a level reminiscent of pillar-like stature. We must return to the values those two massive pillars symbolized. Each of us must re-standardize ourselves to the one and only great truth, and stand behind every word we utter with action.

We've all been created with bronze-like utilitarian substance. We've been designed and able to endure lengthy battles and stand firm, even under great pressure. Men are purposely placed at the gates, at the entrances to the churches of Christ. Every man looking in who wants to know where our faith and standards come from just has to look at what we stand for, the pillars we align ourselves, and then measure himself accordingly.

When we speak what is truth and walk according to those words, these pillars frame the way people come to know Jesus. When you think of it, Jesus is a rightful, steady, and perfectly dependable, two-pillar man. By his flesh He was established in His ministry, and by His divinity He was strong to do what He said He would by fulfilling all what was spoken about Him.

This established him undeniably. He did exactly what he said he would, even unto loss of reputation, even unto death.

What's the size, construction, shape, and capability of the pillars you've placed the weight of your world upon? God is still looking to firmly establish around his temple the solid strength of two-pillar kind of men.

When the weight of right and wrong hang in the balance and need a place to rest, will your pillars be enough? When your own legacy as a man of honor are tested under the microscope of a younger one who is building a foundation from your example, are you Jachin? Will you help to establish something eternal? When it's going to cost you something great to keep a promise or to admit a failing, are you going to be a Boaz, one who has the structural strength of design to bear up?

Will the metallurgy of what your pillars are made from be weighed and measured, and found wanting?

Does your brand of truth have the material substance and girth to bear the kind of weight to support the size of the task to which you were created and called?

It's been said that the true measure of a man is what he would do if he knew he would never by caught. Well, I had gotten caught. I could have "pleaded the fifth" by hiding behind the excuse that I didn't know what happened on the back street on launch day. But the mischievousness of doing something funny, out of bounds, and explosive is the appeal of setting off a gargantuan rocket in the first place, followed by the momentary lapse in critical judgment. In its place, truth, maturity and respect became the casualty that day.

Trying to dodge the initial blast by hiding in the house was wrong, as was by no means my normal, sworn-to practice. The knee-jerk reaction to save face illustrates a point. We're not going to be necessarily seeking out damage we may have caused, but in the future, it might be worthwhile in dealing with airborne ordinance. Hiding only served to shrink me to lesser man status. But fortunately, our God is one of redemption and second chances, and I'd received a blessing that day, an opportunity to become the mass of the man I was created in spite of the initial reaction.

Pillar size. It first attracts attention, but where it matters is the metallurgy. What it's made of, like the man, is the measure that really matters.

DAVID B. LOVEALL

CHAPTER 5 – **CRAMP OR SWIM, THE FIRST PILLAR**

I grew up under the immanent rule of death that I had to wait at least a half-hour before swimming after eating lunch. There were absolutely no cannonballs before the timer went off.

Although the medical science of this has never been proven, it can't be negated. The fact is, by obeying this standard to the very minute, I've never cramped up in the water and therefore I've never come close to drowning, even after bodacious summer rations of PB and J sandwiches and copious cups of Kool-aid.

This law stood as a pillar of truth and life in my youth. It was tested and never crossed. The adherence to it has thankfully gotten me here to tell you about these man-pillar concepts as an adult.

Solid standards do that. Over time, they prove themselves worthy, even if at first they might seem really obvious or superfluously rigorous. Solid morals remain solid when we remain obedient to them. Somewhere the men who witnessed the first temple got loose with their standards. This slackness is what eventually brought on the complete devastation of the grandest temple ever built. The final casualty was the complete dismemberment of the pillar standards of their faith walk.

It happened similarly to the guy who believed a little porn is OK. This same guy swore he was not looking at it on his computer.

The day eventually came when his compromises to the truth had him in my office tearfully admitting that the porn which was destroying him wasn't on his computer, it was on his smart-phone. These kinds of hair-splitting compromises are what lead to total destruction of any pillar a man tries to build as a testament to his own standard of honesty.

Note when the second temple was rebuilt, it didn't even have pillars! Nor did it have the ark of the covenant, the mercy seat or the cherubim, either. In fact, when the priest would enter the second temple, he wasn't framed by the massive reminders of Jehovah's establishing presence nor of his strength from the pillars that stood at the doorway of the first. In the inner most "holiest of holies" where he would perform the sacrifices in grand gold surrounding, one has to realize, the second temple was empty. Some scholars have said the second temple just didn't have the budget of Solomon's. It didn't have the conviction. It was buried in the rubble of shame because it most certainly was an inferior version of the former. Regret is a pillar killer.

Such is the outcome when men practice poor "pillarship." They become inferior to the standard of what they were first created for and then have to live with a plan B version. Each time they rest their words and actions on something lesser, they in turn, become poorer men of character. God doesn't have a plan B for you.

As I write this, many years after standing in the doorway of our home that morning, my son is now 29 years old. He's endured seven years of calculus and engineering school, learned how to navigate his life under the spirit of God with his own oars, and is now married nearly two years to the most incredible woman from a story that in itself, is book worthy. He's an entrepreneur and runs a world-wide business with his wife. He risks, he snowboards, he mentors middle school kids at his church, he follows his faith like it was on steel rails. He believes whole-heartedly in doing the right thing, even when it's exceedingly more difficult than taking the low road to compromise. He's a solid young man, to say the least.

A few years after the rocket incident, while in seventh grade, one of those "never forget" statements popped out of his mouth when I was kidding around with him about not having a girlfriend du jour.

He said, "Dad, I figure it this way, I only have a certain amount of innocence to give away. And if I give it all away now, I won't have any when it's really going to matter."

I remembered those and other stunning words of faith when I found myself years later standing on a barn stage, in the mountains of Oregon, the afternoon of his wedding day. It was my turn (as the father of the groom) to say a few words about what I called the "substance of faith," which highlighted both of theirs.

By this time, he and his wife had journeyed through their own crucibles, discovering individually that God could be trusted through the fires of life. I reminded them by their walks of faith and character under His pillar standards, is what brought them to this next entrance, to the beginning of the lives they both dreamed of. It was those massive, immovable pillars of character they both stuck to that got them through the valleys of despair. The pillars kept them on the narrow way sparing them both when the broad and easier way, would have without doubt destroyed both of them.

I couldn't help but think too, of that fateful rocket day on our front porch. What would denial then have etched upon the heart of a young boy? What could have manifested deep into a 29-year-old man's heart character that could have changed that wedding day? A flaw so obscure, that no one would have been able to pinpoint where it came from. It was a brief scene of life that would have faded into the background, interpreted as a father who didn't stand for what he said, and then included in a spiritual belief that a heavenly father probably wouldn't do what He claimed either.

"So is this your bottle rocket or not?" my neighbor repeated as I dithered.

The red stick and blown cylinder wiggled in front of my face like a hypnotic, dry windshield wiper. I could almost smell the bouquet of consequences. I remembered perfectly the high-pitched scream months ago that afternoon of a woman right after the sonic boom. It sounded serious. Sheesh, why do you think we packed up the launching chute so quickly and got back in the house?

My son was next to the man he called his father, just where all good sons stand at defining moments. He gazed at me, sending again what looked like the signal to duck and dodge. I couldn't tell what he was thinking. But I could tell you the only two thoughts that were running through my conflicted mind.

"Two pillars". And that made everything come into crystal clarity. It was pillar time.

Right here is where rules fail every time. What I'm about to tell you is not a rule. It's a standard of character. It's a practice that promises to build every time it's swung. It's courage on a stick that you can stick to the enemy when he wants to ruin you and those you unwittingly teach by every small decision made.

I can do this, I thought. I can speak the truth. Just move my lips and grab onto **PILLAR NUMBER ONE**: *"Speak the truth. even if the truth leads to your death."*

Speaking the truth isn't just telling the truth as you might see it. That's a concept. It's speaking what *is true*. When I was my son's age, my parents assured me that if I always told the truth when confronted with a choice to lie, I would get in "less trouble". Just what is, "less trouble" going to be? Especially now?

These days, the avoidance of "less trouble" should be our aim considering that lies about anyone can multiply so fast with viral communication, social media and the gossip wheel turning at warp speed. Winston Churchill was a prophet when he said back in the 1940's, "A lie gets halfway around the world before the truth has a chance to put its pants on". Deceitful character from "white" (or any) lies are the leprosy of a man's legacy.

Pillar number one will always establish three truths that will last. Who you are, whom you follow, and whom you serve. Remember, truth is a person. Speaking the truth is what Jesus does and who He is. If He lives inside of you, it's what you do, even (and especially) when you want to do something different to save your own skin. With practice and trust however, it becomes how you live, too.

In the process of eventually adopting our youngest son, William, my wife and I first embarked on getting him here on a student visa. We were empty nesters, the last thing we were looking for was another child on the tax form. From her previous African mission trip, my wife had made a strong connection with this pre-teen and couldn't stop thinking of a way to help him significantly.

Long story short, on our first trip back to Africa, in an attempt to bring him here on U.S. on a student visa, we had to produce in court a relative of William's mother as another source to prove he was an orphan. The advising pastor and lawyer suggested we just get anyone off the street, pay them some money and have them testify.

"This is done here all the time," the pastor said. "It's how we do things in Africa for the greater good."

It took my wife a nano-second to fire back.

"We will not lie. It's not who we are, or what we do, regardless of what that costs us. Even if it costs us William not coming to America."

So we didn't do the little white lie and that move cost us dearly. We ended up fully adopting William but not after I got stuck in Africa a second time for three months, while my wife solely and bravely battled the red tape to get us both back. This is what first pillar speaking does. It establishes who you are and readies you for the next leap of faith into a larger story God has already planned.

Conversely, if you've blown up something and need to fess up, the first pillar doesn't necessarily remove the guilt of an offense getting you off scot-free. We'll all offend. What it does though, is not allow shame and the hypocrisy that latches onto a man's character to become a part of who you are, and more importantly, how others see you. Guilt is what comes from you doing something wrong. Shame comes from you doing nothing about making something right and the wrong becomes part of who you are.

Taking the rocket stick from my neighbor and glancing over it like a forensic nerd, I showed it to my 10-year-old co-conspirator. Pokerfaced, his gelled, flat-top haircut didn't even nod.

Cramping was starting to churn deep down in my gut. Maybe I should have waited a little longer before I decided to swim in that next session. But it was time. The metaphoric half-hour was up. Swim in truth. Or drown in lies.

"Yes, sir," I said unmistakably. "That's unfortunately, my rocket."

I exhaled and handed him back the incriminating evidence.

Jachin had fallen headfirst into the pool. He had established Jehovah's word at this house. What we spoke here was solid. It and us, could be trusted.

So as we stood at the entrance of my porch in that awkward moment of silence for what came right after, I readied myself for the next pillar. Because Boaz was up next.

Cannonball!

CHAPTER 6 – **PAY UP, THE SECOND PILLAR**

"That last line, the one you just spoke requires you to do something, dad-gum it!"

My middle school drama teacher bellowed from the rear of the darkened theater countless times. She called it "necessary action."

"Necessary action" is the movement from the lines (words) spoken from an actor that require compulsory, essential, absolute completion. Without action, the scene wouldn't make sense.

"If you're telling us 'Out, damned spot. Out I say!' And you aren't dealing with the spot, or rubbing your hands in some way, you wouldn't be doing anything you said."

"Do what you say. In doing what you say, it's going to require something from you, necessary action, always remember that," she said.

Our church leader goals for the next year were posted on large easel papers and taped to the foyer walls.

They were a "visual script" to the spoken words at the meeting weeks earlier. These scripts reminded me of those I held in my hand during drama class. There was "necessary action" written all over them. As expected, a number of them were physical, but many were spiritual, too.

Some wanted to lose weight. Physical actions. One guy joked that he wanted his running shoes to get fixed because they were broken. Apparently, he bought them, put them strategically by the front door, but claimed they weren't running even after he told them to get jogging. Spiritual problems more than physical there, eh?

On my own hanging easel paper were "low bar" goals. My wife and I were still adjusting to the year-long ordeal adopting William from Uganda. We were busy up-shifting, playing taxi and being science project parents and algebra tutors. So our goals in my opinion weren't much of a stretch. Not like the beer belly needing to run.

Somewhere down at the bottom of my list, I wrote that I wanted to do 20 chin ups and run a 6:30 mile time. Two physical strengths that were maintenance rather than real stretch goals.

My worship pastor however, was an "ooh-rah", shout-it-out-and –do-it kind of ex-Marine. He'd only been out of the country one time, but blurted out a biggie and wrote it boldly with a black sharpie on the wall paper. He felt God was directing him to go to Uganda to be a part of the men's conference mission trip we were planning for the coming Fall. He daringly proclaimed he was "all in." Since he had spoken words into the spirit arena, those words now had to produce something physical. Follow through. Necessary action. A dose of commitment.

So I contend that there are two kinds of strength increase, physical and spiritual, which are fueled by our words and exercised by our actions. To exercise the spiritual we tend to lean the greatest importance on the words spoken in prayer. But in fact, as we've seen already, **all words** spoken from our mouths are regarded as promises, covenants, and all are expected to be enacted upon with integrity. Even the ones whispered in secret.

As we can see, all words are going to require something from the bodily physique, because they too, are an equally weighty call to action as prayer words are. Just ask the apostle Paul who (spoke the words) to be a voice to distant churches. Those words put great demands on his physical perseverance. He was shipwrecked, beaten, stoned, chained and shackled, suffering for each sentence spoken into the spirit realm, and in the end, faced imprisonment for the sum total of them. The demands of his spiritual growth demanded great bodily participation stemming from his commitments spoken. It cost him dearly.

Just like when my wife and I decided to bring an orphan into America as a student whom she met on a dental mission trip a year earlier. We hired a lawyer and thought we had all the ducks in a row. But once we got into court, the judge threw us a curveball. We had to return and get more support paperwork and home studies to even have a shot. He said only one of us needed to return and so a few months later, I came back on what I thought was going to be a quick 10-day trip.

Because we endured such a heart-wrenching defeat when my wife and I were there months earlier, I spoke a vow to William when I got off the plane December 4 of 2012.

"I made a promise to Nita and I'm making a promise to you young man, I'm not leaving here without you." I said. Little did anyone know what keeping those words with necessary action would turn into. It was nearly March of the next year before we could return. The vow had turned into a full adoption and more importantly, a spiritual connection to Uganda that formed an international ministry. Many times what you think is necessary action for you, physical or spiritual, is only the tip of a much larger story.

I would also challenge the notion that self-espoused physical growth also requires a pound of flesh from the spirit. For example, if I'm going to even think about beating my teenage son in basketball, I better get my spirit will into practicing my long jump shot. If not, my words are nothing more than idle banter, proving I'm a man who can't prove anything. So in reality, strength in one or the other, requires portions from both.

The vat that never gets filled is the one of physical. Men can shovel effort into that bottomless hole our whole lives and never get awarded a badge of honor, much less a blue ribbon. How many points? Touchdowns? Distance? Salary? Car? Or new record high? These are worthy accomplishments, the kind that resonate from a shallow spirit. They all come down to what a man can do, press, lift, navigate, or perform solely for the attention or admiration of those immediately around him. Even if he doesn't realize long-term respect is really what he's after.

The Bible says that every man is called 'holy unto God,' so there must be an arena where ***every man*** can be equally regarded as a first place kind of participant, a place where each man is not only able to succeed, but really excel. In this place, every man can step up to the podium and gain the applause of a lasting legacy. This is where fruit, the kind that remains over a lifetime, comes from the works of his words. Every man who competes and sweats and trains in this stadium of character can be a gladiator.

Paul tells young Timothy, "Exercise daily in God—no spiritual flabbiness, please! Workouts in the gymnasium are useful, but a ***disciplined life in God*** is far more so, making you fit both today and forever. You can count on this. Take it to heart."
(1 Timothy 4:8-9 MSG)

What Paul says here is the muscle of a man that people remember isn't physical prowess. It's the potent asset and dependability of character. It's the reliability of words reaping into a harvest of necessary action. This comes from disciplined workouts of repetition. Speak and do. Promise and finish well.

Therefore, a man bound to a wheelchair can be as notable and strong as a man who jerks a 400-pound barbell off the floor in the Olympics. A janitor at a high school can be just as life-saving as a combat veteran who lost a limb while jumping on a grenade to save a buddy. Why? Because they both may have uttered some concoction of words like, "I got 'yer back", "I'll be there when I said I would". They both have pre-decided to keep their words even before the situation comes about to test them on their actions.

'Live to Tell' is a show on the History channel. It's stories about young men in life and death situations during combat in Iraq and Afghanistan. On one episode, an Explosive Ordinance guy was imbedded with the Army Rangers. His job was to walk ahead of the squad using his trained sense of IED's (improvised explosive devices) to detect and disarm hidden bombs meant to kill the people who depended on him. But who had his back?

"I depend on the snipers behind me to use their scopes and to take out threats they see ahead and around me," he said. "Knowing they have my back takes the worry off so I can cover the backs to my brothers who follow after me."

The EOD guy stakes his life on the word of someone who, in turn, stakes their life on him. That's how warriors work in the battle. That's how we warriors need to work in this battle.

There's nothing stronger than a man's word. Fancy contracts can't reinforce what cunning lawyers can unravel by omission of what was spoken and not signed. But it shouldn't matter. Extra emphases or phrases like, "I swear by those words" attached to promises doesn't make any of them stronger. A man's word, that which has fallen from his lips, is a covenant the Bible tells us. An iron-clad promise. Lives depend on it in the grand scheme of things. Those utterances in the ear shot of God are unbreakable vows and also should be to the hearer, unless, death by one of the parties makes it impossible. A man's word and the yearning to keep and perform it is the only force that doesn't decline when age and vigor decrease. Each man can become better every time he passes through these entrances of opportunity.

The second pillar of the temple, Boaz, means "in strength". This is the defining pillar of this next bronze-fired principle.

Biblical man names, like that of Boaz, historically come from a number of sources. Tradition, nation, revelations, prophecies, circumstances at birth time or most often, special meaning pertaining to character of what was hoped for by the giving the name.

Take the story of Boaz and Ruth, told in the book of Ruth. Right out of the gate it shows us Boaz as the strong man of principle. Initially, we see him as a speaker of truth when he greets his workers every morning with "The Lord (Jehovah) be with you". To which his workers replied "The Lord bless you". (Ruth

2:4 NKJ) He was known throughout his region as a man of authority, integrity, faith, self-control, kindness, generosity and a resolute man of action. He did what he said and didn't dally about it when action was required.

As we zip through the story toward the end, Boaz is faced with the customary opportunity to buy back the mother in-law's property of her dead husband, but also in the deal, must take Ruth as a wife per tradition. The next of kin was solely responsible for this act of word, spoken within the family, insuring that the property, inheritance and rights would remain within the family. Boaz was a close relative but he wasn't the very next one in line to do exercise this duty. The night Boaz found Ruth sleeping at his feet he connected the dots on this potential liability, or opportunity of keeping his word (however you wish to see it). We note that the very next morning, he took immediate action on his responsibilities to the family name.

Boaz had put forth this assurance to Ruth in the darkness of the previous night saying, *"But while it's true that I am one of your family redeemers, there is another man who is more closely related to you than I am. Stay here tonight, and in the morning I will talk to him. If he is willing to redeem you, very well. Let him marry you. But if he is not willing, then as surely as the Lord lives, I will redeem you myself! Now lie down here until morning."*
(Ruth 3:12-13 NLT)

Boaz made a hefty and costly promise, especially when he could have said he was too busy during harvest season to be bothered with such a disruptive issue. It's worth mentioning here that he also protected her virtuous reputation by not acting upon his own preferences in the moment. Remember, available women were considered convenient property for man's amusement and pleasure. But Boaz's character was always first to be focused on doing what was right, regardless of the outcome to him. This is classic, unselfish honor.

If Ruth was to become his wife, there would be honor in doing it properly. If she was to be purchased back into the family by another man, he took it upon himself to make sure there was honor in that as well. It didn't matter those words were in the wee hours of the night, which were not only heard between Boaz, and Ruth, but also by his God.

The next morning, Boaz gets the necessary men to do some formal contract sandal swapping. At the critical moment though, when the closest relative was identified and given his opportunity to redeem what could have been his, he instead took back his word on repurchasing the land of Naomi's husband. Basically the deal was not going to be good for his bottom line. The cost was high. It was about him. It was a major inconvenience for him to keep that kind of word. Always is.

Does the "idea" of keeping your word always seems like a "slam dunk"? Because unless it requires something greater of you, like a little more sacrifice, dealing with might seem like a nuisance, or even a hit on the fragile reputation a man has created around himself, it's nothing more than making an easy lay-in. Boaz wasn't concerned with any of those. He viewed his word as the treasure of his character, worth the cost, worth the continued investment.

He purchased the land, took Ruth as a wife and through his lineage, Jesus Christ came. Unimaginable blessings come from character like this. That's always been God's promise to his men.

The instant I told my neighbor the rocket scraps were mine the three of us at the doorway nervously chuckled. Just like they do in the movies when the tension of drawing guns and shooting each other passes.

I'm certain the guy came to my house knowing that I was going to deny everything and weasel out of the predicament somehow on a technicality. Certainly he had already predisposed to leave empty-handed and only receive a flippant kind of "F.U.," adding to the sum total of the disappointing integrity of mankind. Or he thought that some sort of chest-bumping posture was going to have to come to play to strong arm the truth outa' me. Who really knows?

The confession of truth from me ushered in the second phase of the perfectly effective, pillar architecture. Now that truth was spoken, the word of Jehovah was firmly established. What comes next is the all important "in strength" part. And all of us had a potential workout in that coming.

Pillar number two can, at times, be tougher than the truth. It's the muscle that works to make things right. It closes the gap when often times that span is large.

PILLAR NUMBER 2 is simply this: *Do what you say. Even if doing what you say costs you dearly.*

Without missing a beat, my neighbor went right on to testing my resolve on this second pillar. The two pillars are intricately connected. They're a pair of supports. One can't exist without the other. They bear equal weight. The roof of the temple needed the complete design structure and mass of both pillars. The shelter of heaven can't be supported by a man who just speaks truth. The Bible says faith (truth) without works (strength in action) is dead. In this architecture reference, utter demolition.

I've lived in my house nearly twenty-five years. By now I've got a certain reputation about the neighborhood. But don't we all? Yours could be the guy who drives the cool car, or the smartly dressed businessman, or suburban jerk who power-washes his driveway until midnight every Spring, or the weirdo who keeps to himself, or the guy who never rakes up his leaves until just before Christmas. Whatever. All of the reputations we make for ourselves are temporary stage curtains of weaker character. God doesn't want us to be seen by 'reputations', but as 'replications' of His character. This is legacy. Legacy costs. Every time we keep our word, we have the divine occasion to build on that. It's our own legacy in reflecting Christ in us.

That recreational rocket had done some real and billable damage. When you bear truth, often it uncovers damage that you didn't know existed but still needs your complete and thorough attention. Even though the rocket went off radar almost instantly after being lit out of our chute, my neighbor wasn't on my doorstep to talk about flight specifics, or missed trajectories. He was there to address all of the collateral damages, of which, were ignited by me.

My neighbor continued to fill me in on the full extent to the rockets sudden splash down.

"When I got home from vacation I found my son-in-law had boarded up my dining room window for me." I sighed. Window out, that's bad. I felt the other Shaq-sized court shoe was about to drop, right on my wallet.

"When your rocket hit my dining room window, it shattered the glass from corner to corner all the way across the frame. It blew powder burns up the side of my house into the roof eaves, and once it penetrated the window, it burned itself out on my wood floor spinning sparks all over the room. I found this stick under my wife's china cabinet." Suddenly, I was thankful the wife wasn't there to hurdle my back fence and beat me with a rolling pin.

Without admitting anything further, (like I had to), all I could say was, "Uh. Wow. "

Then crickets. Just before the next set of words between us, would become vows of action. I braced myself.

"I tell you what," he bargained using the red rocket stick as a laser pointer. "I'm a contractor, and if you just pay me for the cost of a new window, I will install it and we can call this all even."

"Deal!" I said without hesitation. That seemed like the bargain of a lifetime and if I didn't jump on it immediately, that baby just might have evaporated from indecisiveness. I mean how much could a side house window cost, right? Apparently, way more than I was expecting.

"That window is a six by four foot insulated vinyl window. I just put one in at a remodel job I was working before I left for vacation. I remember it costing right at $250 dollars," he said.

Ouch! Based on the scope of his damage report, I could've been facing accidental arson and two-hundred and fifty thousand! This was a good deal right at this moment, especially if he wasn't going to be looking around at other potential damages. This is the part where if one doesn't keep one's word right the heck now, it can have diminishing value of the cost you've decided to face.

We'd settled on the damages all right, but my reaction speed was going to dictate the overall restoration of my character. It's like when someone asks you to pray for them after telling you a gut-wrenching story in the beer aisle of the store. Praying isn't what you normally do while holding a six-pack of sudsy hops, so you give an intentionally goodwill promise to the requester to pray later. And after a few brewski's and a football game, you summarily forget. That me bucko…is a broken vow, plain and simple. Your word to heal your friend and to stand in the gap for him was ultimately, worthless. Even though your intentions were of the highest caliber, the doing simply slipped your mind and didn't get done. We've all done it.

"Let me get my checkbook and take care of that right now," I said, dashing to the bill drawer in the kitchen and grabbing a black pen, scratching the draft.

At my age, I may never maintain a 20 chin ups a year quota. My muscles will most likely atrophy to advancing years and with each passing birthday. What's in my future? The senior discount on Denny's grand slam breakfast, then Medicare and Social Security checks, then, well, the inevitable. Depends, or sport trunks. Whatever.

But there's one mighty power you and I can both do to continue building on clear to the grave. The strength of keeping words.

Right there, at my door, in front of my son, I scrawled a check for a broken window of which I never saw. I handed it to my neighbor whom I didn't know, and apologized for the inconvenience and damage I caused beyond the window. We shook hands firmly, mutually, respectfully.

I believe because the truth was spoken and followed by doing what was vowed, at the soonest "git-r-done', God restored something very valuable to my families inheritance. Like Boaz, this situation gave opportunity to repurchase back assets that could have died or been buried under deceit. Assets the enemy knew were supposed to be kept within my family. Things like honor, integrity, fairness, compassion, truth, and charity. Things of substance that puts medals on a family crest.

A man's kept word extends benefits beyond his own family borders. It heals brokenness with others and restores what could have become adversarial relationships. It builds foundations of knowledge and impressionable examples into the legacy of young men who are watching and learning.

During a conversation with a religious leader, Jesus asked how he read the laws of Moses. Rules to right. How much real responsibility does a man have to do, to be right toward another man? The man answered resolutely from his mind, *"You must love the Lord your God with all your heart, all your soul, all your strength, and all your mind.' And, 'Love your neighbor as yourself."*

"Right!" Jesus told him. "Do this and you will live!"

(Luke 10:27-28 NLT)

But if a man says he loves (the laws of the Lord) and doesn't do the necessary actions to obey them with his life, or picks and chooses the one's that suit his shifting values, then he's building a structure with flimsy pillars that are certain to crumble. By ignoring these two vital standards, he's not ever going to gain full entrance into the holiest of places with God. Without even knowing it, he's even closing the doors for those who are looking to him to show the way also.

The true cost of that day wasn't $250 bucks. It was the potential price tag of what any other set of pillars might have been charged against one ten-year-old boy.

I actually wrote the check for him, so that my display of character, faith, and trust in my God, would be an immovable witness to something he could align himself with. A pillar that at any cost, would hold fast for the rest of his life, even if the timing of this pillar display of action was caused by a forced course correction.

Life is doing the necessary action, *live*. After all, this isn't middle school play rehearsal.

CHAPTER 7 – **THE GOSPEL OF THE ROCKET STORY**

The next day after the porch drama, was the start of Saturday college football bowl games. With everyone glued to the tube for their favorite college game opener, the window at my neighbor's house was being replaced. I could hear the hammering and sawing from my back deck

He did the installation just like he said he would. All vows completed. Honor, integrity, respect, and two pillars still standing in the neighborhood. I sipped my coffee with sweeter spiritual satisfaction than the caramel creamer offered.

Even to this day, a few decades later, that same neighbor still waves at me nearly every time I drive by. I still don't know his name. But he knows mine, because he shouts it out after each wave. To be fair, he never told me his name. Mine was on the check for two-and-a-half Franklins.

The thing I still scratch my head about is that he makes it a point to notice me. If the situation would've turned out under fraudulent circumstances, I'm sure the only communication would have been an artificial ignoring of one another. He would have been understandably bitter. If it was me, I would have carried some sort of juvenile snigger under my breath celebrating the fact that I got away with something that I really shouldn't have. In every other circle that's called sin, not entertainment at the expense of someone else. The sad thing is, in a self-made parallel universe with all of my own laws working only in my favor, I would've blindly believed that I was still an honorable and honest kind of guy. The window/rocket story would have been covered under the humor of the event and ended up being somehow justified as an irresponsible error that I wasn't responsible for. My perception would've concluded that the ding to my honor armor wasn't significant enough in the grand scheme of things to worry about. I would have been dead wrong.

Thankfully, that rocket-chip to the honor was checked at my door. Just like yours will be every time the pillar tests are standing in your entryways. Especially the ones at the gate to holiness where many people stand looking to you first to see if they see any shreds of God. The pillars bring that out of every man by design. It's God's design. The work they produce in you might be relatively unseen until the steady process shows up as fruit in someone else's life who has tested the principles while watching you live them.

At first I started telling the Rocket Story at parties just for a few laughs as a "one-up" example about how I really could have blown something. It then came into my home for men's group as an icebreaker. Slowly it began popping onto the pages of a few sermons as an illustration about honest principles and how even the smallest of mindless fibs, can take root in large ways in the minds of our kids. Then God started showing me the connection the story had to the temple pillars. Once I deciphered what they stood for, their grand statements became a constant staple in my life to measure against any compromising threat that would have me ducking out of what God wanted me to face. The two-pillar man teaching then found itself in many more man topics taught in church weekend encounters and even the chapels of local prisons.

Fast forward. From that fateful mission trip my wife went on ended up being one of the greatest stories of our lives, something else was born from that first failed trip. A grand ministry. While waiting for the first court dates, the pastor in charge of the orphanage and I put together a two-day men's conference for his church men.

Based on what my wife told me from her first trip and from other missionaries, I gathered that the local Ugandan men needed some basic tools. The large majority of the men needed to be taught the milk of basic integrity and what it looks like day to day. They needed to know that if there was a bicycle leaning against a house, that it wasn't God's answer to prayer that they could take it for their own transportation. The simple, yet weighty pillar principles that were catching fire here in the U.S. was an unknown in this other culture and country. I didn't know how the pillars would translate, but I felt the strong spirit to teach it. Besides, I had two full days of other "man topics" planned anyway, so I buried the teaching early in the second day just in case it flopped.

It struck gold. One man in particular, a Kenyan pastor named Edward Mbuyi, crept in late that second morning. He had already missed the first day entirely, but was taking diligent notes from the front row all morning. Come to find out, this "pastor" (only one of his vocations apparently) had missed the first day because he's also the village garbage man. He had his refuse route the day prior so he could collect enough funds to get the gas money to come to the conference.

At the lunch break he was introduced to me by an American missionary friend. We were staying at their house during the trip and Edward, coincidently, was this guy's garbage collector.

The garbage man/pastor was visibly excited about the two pillar lesson. He showed me his notes like a grade-school kid who just spelled his name correctly. Scrawled across the top single page were a couple of lines. They were the pillar sentences in large letters written over a couple of times to make them bolder.

"Pastor David," he says rubbing his buzz-cut scalp and brown forehead. "These principles are changing my life as we speak. They are an answer to much prayer and personal struggle."

"How so?" I asked. "It isn't even lunch time."

Edward proceeded to give me his forty year life story and how at this critical juncture, he was looking for something solid to set his sail through the choppy waters of faith he found himself in.

Long story short, he was now submitting to being sent to Uganda by the call of God. For the past 12 years he lived (like Jonah avoiding the ministry) in England working as a baggage handler at Heathrow airport. He could be called a responsible, but absent father. He had just moved to Uganda to finally answer that call of ministry but without his family. He was wrestling with a crucial piece of his manhood, the promise to be a father. He said he realized that morning that his father role was still left un-acted upon. His boys were growing up without his influence, and it had been haunting him.

He was typical. In many cultures, an absent dad makes money enough for his family to survive, but lives marginalized to his man calling. His two young sons were quickly coming out of boyhood and starting to ask those tough questions about their missing father who just sent money from abroad. They were tough life questions that if not learned properly, become substitute lesser pillars in the way they choose to model themselves as men in the future.

In Edward's self constructed universe, he still saw himself as a man of integrity. He was a financial pillar, providing steady chicken and matokee money. However, in the boys minds, and in his wife's too, the rest of his manhood contracts were grossly in default. They were being scrutinized with anger and judgment by his sons because Edward's words were those dangerous, empty-of-action kinds of words.

The very next day, after the conference, he decided to go immediately back to Kenya, gather up his family, and move them to Uganda to be with him. He took a huge leap of faith to trust God with the rest. He said taking that leap in keeping his true word was more important than sending schilling notes home with an absently sincere message. He was determined to being a two-pillar man, dad, and husband from that point on.

"I knew the moment you spoke those two pillars into my heart, man, I knew that I was not a man of my word." he said looking back to that day, now some four years later.

"In just a few months time, after my sons and family were with me, they witnessed the shift and favor God was doing in me and the ministry. Plus the changes He was doing in me as a man," Edward said as his voice started to crack. "My oldest boy said one day as we were collecting the garbage at the homes of all the missionaries here in town, 'Dad, someday I want to be a man like you'. Man, I tell you David, those pillars changed my life forever and put life changing seed into my family!"

I can look back on that day and know for certain that God brought Edward and I together. We are now forever linked. We're now partners in a global ministry in Uganda. He is a dear friend. A prophetic and trusted brother. Two Pillars built that.

Speak the truth, even if the truth leads to your death. Do what you say. Even if doing what you say costs you dearly. These principles that changed this one pastor have begun to change a nation through him and countless others who have adopted these columns of character to their Christianity.

A few months after the conference, when I had returned for what I thought was going to be the "slam-dunk" visit to bring William home as a student, I was the one faced with keeping man words. That promise I made to William earlier, about not leaving without him, required another pound of flesh.

After quickly gaining legal guardianship, we went to the VISA office to leave a few days later and get back home with him by Christmas. I pulled the famous last words to my wife when I left the airport that was straight out of the movie Cast Away, when I yelled back, "Don't worry, I'll be right back". Once at the VISA window however, I found I couldn't bring him into the U.S. due to bad legal immigration advice. Unbeknownst to us, there was a mound of red tape we never knew about. All told, I was delayed in Africa for three months. Why?

Because I told my would-be-son when I arrived at the airport, "This time, I promised your mom and now I'm promising you, I'm not going to leave with out you." Those words meant everything to him, and the cost to those words were more than my wife and I could've ever imagined.

Yet, during that time, many moves of God were set into motion. Opportunities to minister and set up a trusted ally in another country took root. Edward and I became hands-on pastors to the region and active teachers of the two pillars principles. We both became living illustrations. Both of us became known as two pillar men wherever we spoke. It caught a fire in the local men that we never could've predicted.

From that tiny spark of fiery spirit and partnership, so far we have built two churches, been partners in an orphanage with several outbuildings, constructed Edward's personal home, raised a strong group of fellow visionaries who send funds to feed a few hundred children, and personally trained over 500 men and women in conferences. And still counting. We're even finding inroads to putting together a medical clinic in a remote valley. The two pillars are the architect details of everything the Lord chooses to build through each of us.

Edward has heard the rocket story told dozens of times from me. Each instance he hears me say the introductory words, "I want to talk about two pillars", he readjusts himself on his chair, readying himself for the laughs and the resonance of what's coming. *The rocket story.*

"David, I tell you man," he says with that African Rastafarian brogue laughing with all of his belly, "Wherever the gospel is preached, the rocket story must be told!"

To that I say to every man, may the rocket story remind all men that if they're going to blow stuff up, don't destroy the truth for the sake of hiding your responsibilities or shielding some fragile reputation. Don't demolish the dependability of your words by using them to give people what they want to hear, but never following up on the actions they expect.

Don't miss the opportunities to test the two pillars even in the most gristly gripping of man life. They work. They're able to stand with the heaviest of loads. By their design, they will be the entrance that brings you into the place you belong.

What you stand to lose if you don't stand as the pillar of a man God designed you for, are chances; chances for reconciliation, restoration, peace within your borders. You purpose, legacy and most of all, something no man on the planet can live without; respect...the kind that goes deep, and remains for a lifetime.

What kind of man to you want to be? Loftier still, what kind of man do you want your son to be if you've already vowed to be a father? Sadly, over the last 200 years, men have passed on less and less to their sons. Our legacy to be men of character who raise men of character is steadily dying. There is less moral wisdom, less spiritual power, less love and sacrifice for one another, less foundation of truth, which all contribute to men with less faith in themselves and the God who is supposed to be in them.

Truth is, God hasn't stopped working at depositing good things into ordinary men who will become great men. We are still His workmanship, and to my knowledge, He hasn't stopped working on any of us. So it's not His fault. It's ours. We have become less than fully committed to a simple, yet powerfully aligning set of principles designed to hold the door of the temple open for us and to others wishing to enter in. They're a grand symbol to remind all men that we are key supports to the church of Christ. We are His leaders, elders, deacons, and hands that serve the sheep for His glory.

With such a calling of honor, I can't help but wonder why there's such an increasing fear in being a real man. And why there is such a resistance to fully engage with our sons who will one day succeed us. Is it because of our wounds? Or the fear that we may be honestly discovered for who we really are? Yet even with all of the facades uncovered, men can still do this. The two pillars are solid, offering a growth foundation that every man can latch onto at any stage. They are valuable, and worthy to emulate. These pillars will dependably lead all men into the presence of holy places, through valleys of challenge and despair and threats of compromise or temptations to hide in the house.

Men don't lack incentive. We can find incentive in anything if it seems to feed that insatiable, empty hole in us. What men lack is simple permission. Permission to fail and recover and then really succeed at something that matters. Who ever said we could at any point of failure, gain back real respect after losing face? God! He will boldly rise up and groom us along the way. God has appointed you, now pursue Him. There is your permission.

Men don't lack a compass to truth, either. There's a constant search in every man for truth, but it must be found in the person of Jesus Christ. Grace is larger than your sin. He forgives you and wants you now. Turn around and take a step toward Him, as you speak the words, "make me the man you imagined".

But on top of all, what we men all really hunger for at the deepest spiritual level is for *anointment*. God is ready to drop his oil on us all, because he has paid the full cost to do so.

E.M. Bounds said, *"What the Church needs today is not more machinery or better, not new organizations or more and novel methods, but men whom the Holy Spirit can use... The Holy Spirit does not flow through methods but through men. He does not come upon machinery but on men. He does not anoint plans, but men..."*

When men are anointed by God's Holy Spirit we get the power our soul craves to act in a way that elevates His glory. Acts 1:8 says, *"you will receive power when the Holy Spirit comes upon you."*

The power or the will to have my heart stolen by Uganda was never on my list. But it was on God's. He needed me to be a man of my word because I needed to see Him as a man of his. Through great cost to my self-made stage play, He let me step into what He had waiting for me all this time. I would have never seen it without immovable pillars keeping me in line to receive it.

All of men's seeking is initially about righting our compasses. We need to put aside all the smoke screens and excuses and get back to basic building standards. *Speaking truth and doing what we say.* Our anointing will then come by daily discipline, following both of these emblems of strength and uprightness, as we practice being two-pillar men in a world full of temporary posts.

Though perfectly thought out, the pillars don't cease their effectiveness if they aren't perfectly carried out each and every time. They're a framework to bring a man closer to the heart of God, one life play at a time, even if a man makes some fumbles along the way.

One Fall Saturday afternoon, William, my son from Uganda, sat down to watch our home town college team play a much higher ranked opponent. He told me of his simple plan for our team to win. In a perfect world, the theory would have worked, but in the real world, impossible, the plan destined to fail.

"If our team scores every time they get the football, they'll for sure win, in fact they will always win, including this really tough game," he said.

All you armchair quarterbacks are saying the same thing I'm thinking right now, 'That's just not possible'. Excusing an obvious lopsided exception, no team has every put up points in every possession of a game. And neither do the best of men.

What makes a win possible is when a team and a man overcome playing field mistakes, and capitalize on the opponent's weaknesses. Then fight back hard to score as many times as they can. And when the going gets tough, and the pain of battle sets in, and the costs become high, they don't lose heart. Quitters, and those of the faint-hearted, never win.

Green Bay Packer's coach Vince Lombardi's famous quote still rings true, "Winners never quit and quitters never win. When the going gets tough, the tough get going". Truth doesn't quit. The man Jesus, doesn't quit on any man. Doing what you say, even though tough, will get a man to victory. Those victories are always just past what a man thinks is impossible.

Having two pillars as your permanent principle game plan and life framework won't guarantee you'll always win every game or down. But what it will do is keep you firmly in line for consistent victory (bowl eligible, if you will). You will become more fit, more available, more able to be used by God for more of the most important plays of eternity that include you.

Don't ever give up on being a two-pillar man of character. God made you one, so be one. He stands alongside you in each and every challenge and at the entrance of something potentially grand and glorious, to bring you closer to what you were called to be.

If you make companionship with the likes of Jachin and Boaz, start building a life that's framed around the solid framework of what those two pillars represent, and grab onto the tooled statements that stand up to every situation, you'll soon find yourself respected, a man of stout integrity and standing in solid bronze kind of company.

Speak the truth, even if the truth leads to your death.
Do what you say, even if doing what you say costs you dearly.

For a man, who wants to be a solid fixture of character wherever he stands, these are two proven tools that will fix just about anything.

Become a Two Pillar Man.

Especially, when you blow stuff up.

This book is a tribute to this **TWO PILLAR MAN,** Pastor Edward Mbuyi. If God hadn't moved him closer to the mark, I might have missed it myself.

"Every time and wherever the gospel is preached, the rocket story must be told," says my brother and ministry partner.

Love that guy.

BLESSINGS,

Made in the USA
San Bernardino, CA
13 April 2016